SUMMARY
of
THE SUBTLE ART OF NOT GIVING A F*CK

A Counterintuitive Approach to Living a Good Life

by Mark Manson

A FastReads Book Summary with Key Takeaways & Analysis

Copyright © 2016 by FastReads. All rights reserved. This book or parts thereof may not be reproduced in any form, stored in any retrieval system, or transmitted in any form by any means—electronic, mechanical, photocopy, recording, or otherwise—without prior written permission of the publisher, except as provided by United States of America copyright law. This is an unofficial summary.

TABLE OF CONTENTS

EXECUTIVE SUMMARY 4
CHAPTER 1: DON'T TRY 5

The Feedback Loop from Hell

The Subtle Art of Not Giving a Fuck

So Mark, What the Fuck Is the Point of This Book Anyway?

CHAPTER 2: HAPPINESS IS A PROBLEM 8

The Misadventures of Disappointed Panda

Happiness Comes from Solving Problems

Emotions are Overrated

Choose Your Struggle

CHAPTER 3: YOU ARE NOT SPECIAL 10

Things Fall Apart

The Tyranny of Exceptionalism

B-b-b-but, if I'm not going to be Special or Extraordinary, what's the Point?

CHAPTER 4: THE VALUE OF SUFFERING 13

The Self-Awareness Onion

Rock Star Problems

Shitty Values

Defining Good and Bad Values

CHAPTER 5: YOU ARE ALWAYS CHOOSING 16

The Choice

The Responsibility/Fault Fallacy

Responding to Tragedy

Genetics and the Hand We're Dealt

Victimhood Chic

There is No "How"

CHAPTER 6: YOU'RE WRONG ABOUT EVERYTHING (BUT SO AM I) — 19

Architects of our Beliefs

Be Careful What You Believe

The Dangers of Pure Certainty

Manson's Law of Avoidance

Kill Yourself

How to Be a Little Less Certain of Yourself

CHAPTER 7: FAILURE IS THE WAY FORWARD — 22

The Failure/Success Paradox

Pain is Part of the Process

The "Do Something" Principle

CHAPTER 8: THE IMPORTANCE OF SAYING NO — 24

Rejection Makes Your Life Better

Boundaries

How to Build Trust

Freedom through Commitment

CHAPTER 9: … AND THEN YOU DIE — 26

Something Beyond Our Selves

The Sunny Side of Death

EXECUTIVE SUMMARY

In this captivating guide, Mark Manson explores how people can achieve practical enlightenment by identifying and prioritizing what is important and, more than that, choosing to not care for frivolities. In his view, the current psychological epidemic is a symptom of people who care too much about the trivialities of life and who have not learned to embrace the inevitabilities of life: failure, suffering, and death. He contends that only by letting go, taking responsibility, and adopting values that are immediate and within control can one live a meaningful life.

Manson offers a refreshing take on the value of adversity, pain, and suffering and goes to show why positive thinking is a self-defeating strategy. He argues that a good, happy life is not a life devoid of problems but a life dotted by problems that one enjoys solving. Only by consciously selecting what to care about, what to struggle for, and what pain to endure can one make the most of his or her life.

CHAPTER 1: DON'T TRY

The narrative of any great inspirational film – in which the protagonist works a low-paying job and lives in shambles but works tirelessly on his craft until he strikes fame or fortune – is the quintessential American dream. Charles Bukowski, who lived as a deadbeat, drunk, and chronic gambler until he became a famed author well into his fifties, epitomizes this dream. However, unlike the romanticized inspirational film, his efforts did not pay off because of a deep sense of determination that saw him through all the rejection letters he received from editors; he became successful because he knew and embraced the fact that he was a failure. He was honest about his worst qualities, and he was upfront about his weaknesses even in his writing.

In a culture that sets unrealistically high expectations on wealth, health, happiness, popularity, and just about any other aspect of life, it is difficult to embrace failure as Bukowski did. Ironically, fixating on the high expectations that you have to meet becomes a constant reminder of everything that is lacking in your life; it becomes a daily mnemonic of the failure you are trying to avoid.

The media and everyone around you is constantly programming you to pursue more of everything because conventional wisdom dictates that more is the key to a better life. Yet a constant want of more or better electronics, vacations, or other materials only leads to an endless pursuit of satisfaction at the expense of your mental health. A good, satisfying life hinges on your ability to care about less and to prioritize only that which is true, important, and immediate.

The Feedback Loop from Hell

Getting anxious about your anxiety or getting angry because of your frequent bouts of anger may feel like a feedback loop from hell, but it is part of being human. The human brain is special in that it is conscious and can think about and react to its own thoughts. Popular culture has propagated the idea that fear, guilt, anxiety, or any other negative emotion is not okay. Consequently, a person experiencing these emotions tends to engage in self-loathing, rather than brush them off as part of life.

Life is less satisfying when you feel bad about feeling bad. Learning to be comfortable with your shortcomings not only keeps the feedback loop from hell in check, but also saves you a lot of agony because you accept that the world is nowhere near perfect. When you stop caring about feeling bad, you stop hating yourself for feeling bad.

As global affluence increases, the human crisis shifts from the material to the spiritual. Levels of stress, anxiety, depression, and other mental problems continue to rise despite the fact almost everyone in a developed country can afford a good life. Paradoxically, the desire for more positive experiences is the cause of a negative life experience. Accepting your negative experiences is a positive experience because it liberates you by taking your focus from what is not right in your life.

You become truly happy only when you stop pursuing happiness, and you begin living when you stop trying to find the meaning of life. Contrary to what one may think, shifting focus away from looks, possessions, feelings, or dreams does not forestall action or lessen ambition. You do something better when you stop caring about the outcome, and you make meaningful achievements when you face your insecurities and embrace negative experiences.

Most people care too much about things they shouldn't care about: a cancelled TV show, a rude store attendant, or unappreciative coworkers. Yet, everyone has a limited time alive, and there's only so much one can care about. Not giving a fuck means choosing what matters most to your life (based on innate personal values), prioritizing it, and quitting your obsessions about everything else. It is a daunting and lifelong struggle, but it may very easily be the only struggle that matters.

Caring about everyone and everything is a sickness: it is an irrational obsession marked by a pressing need to have things in one's way. When you care about everything, you invite suffering to your life because you tend to take every inconvenience personally and you see every difficulty as an injustice.

The Subtle Art of Not Giving a Fuck

Not giving a fuck does not mean adopting an indifferent attitude; it means being comfortable with your imperfections. Indifference is usually borne out of a fear of what others think; it is an attitude self-pitying people use to hide in gray areas. Caring about things is ingrained in human nature. Ultimately, it is not a question of *if* you care about things; it is a question of *what* you care about. Not giving a fuck means doing what you feel is right or important without fearing what other people think or how they will react. It is the willingness to face adversity and embarrassment, to pursue your truth, and to pay the price of being an outcast if it comes to it. It is caring only about family, friends, purpose, and the other things that matter.

If you find yourself caring too much about everything, chances are you don't have much going in your life that you can really care about. So long as you don't have a worthwhile purpose, you will care about every trivial thing that happens.

From birth, people are always choosing what to care about. You become selective about the things you care about as you grow up and mature. As you approach the middle ages, your identity takes shape and you accept the things about yourself that you didn't like. Being comfortable with your flaws and the things you will never achieve is liberating because it allows you to care for the things that truly matter.

So Mark, What the Fuck Is the Point of This Book Anyway?

This book is a guide for finding the things that matter in life and those that don't. It is a reminder that it's normal for things not to work out sometimes, because the belief that inadequacy is not okay is the cause of the current psychological epidemic. Not giving a fuck is about reorganizing your priorities and focusing on what's important because no matter what you do, there will always be loss, failure, and regret. This book is a guide to embracing suffering and letting go.

Key Takeaways

• Not giving a fuck means being comfortable with your shortcomings, finding what is important and meaningful, and choosing to only care for what really matters.

• The pursuit of positive experiences is a negative experience because it is a constant reminder of everything you are not or don't have. Pursuing pain, adversity, and other negative experiences is what makes positive experiences.

CHAPTER 2: HAPPINESS IS A PROBLEM

Regardless of your social or economic status, life is but a form of suffering; people with riches, families, and ambitions suffer because of these things, and people without these things suffer because of their lack. While all suffering is not equal, everyone endures it. As the Buddha – who was raised in opulence as a prince but escaped the palace to find the meaning of life – found out, pain and loss is inevitable; there is no point in trying to resist it.

Dissatisfaction and suffering are not only part of the human condition, but they also play crucial roles in the journey to happiness. Happiness is not an equation you solve by putting all the right pieces together. The assumption that one can work for or earn happiness is the root of most of human suffering.

The Misadventures of Disappointed Panda

Suffering serves a critical biological purpose in that it inspires change. Only through dissatisfaction and insecurity can the human race work to make things better and survive. The constant desire to want something out of reach is what forces the species to press on for more. Pain, on its part, is not an inconvenience; it is an integral part of human nature that teaches one to understand and respect the body's physical or psychological limitations. A life without a healthy dose of pain and suffering is a life detached from the reality of the world. Since life is made up of a series of problems, the best one can do is hope for better problems.

Happiness Comes from Solving Problems

Happiness is a form of endless action in that it comes from continually solving problems. Avoiding or wishing for the absence of problems does not create happiness as problems are a constant in life. Finding the solution to one problem often creates another problem. In this sense, true happiness comes from having and solving problems you enjoy. The problems you solve could be as simple as finding the food you enjoy or as complicated as mending a relationship with someone close to you.

Happiness deludes most people because they deny the presence of their problems – and subsequently avoid confronting them by distracting themselves – or they adopt a victim mentality and convince themselves that the solution is beyond their ability.

Emotions are Overrated

Emotions are nothing more than a mechanism that the body uses to guide you to make beneficial change. Negative emotions remind you that you have unresolved problems, while positive emotions are rewards for taking beneficial action. Emotions are meant to guide, not define, your life. Still, they serve as a vital guide. People who repress emotions make their lives momentous struggles. Likewise, people who overly identify with their emotions struggle because emotions are always changing. A job or partner that makes you happy today tends to be the source of your anger and frustration in the future.

Choose Your Struggle

Everyone wants an easy and glamorous life: to have the perfect job, makes lots of money, and have an admirable social standing. However, most people fail to recognize that the way life turns out depends on the struggles and pains one is willing to endure. Happiness, like any other lifelong achievement, requires one to consciously choose and manage the struggles that matter. Success requires one to appreciate and face the risks, uncertainties, and inconveniences that come with the journey.

"What determines your success isn't, "What do you want to enjoy?" The relevant question is, 'What pain do you want to sustain?' The path to happiness is a path full of shitheaps and shame."

Ultimately, it is what you are willing to struggle through that defines you. You can't love the summit – whether for you this means success, fame, or a good life – without loving and investing in the journey because life does not work that way. It is the people who enjoy grueling hours at the office or gym that rise to the top of the corporate ladder or run and win triathlons.

Key Takeaways

• Pain and suffering are an inherent part of human nature. The best you can do is embrace your current suffering and work towards having better problems because happiness comes from solving problems you enjoy.

• The vision of your triumph is not what determines your success; it is the pain you choose and are willing to endure and enjoy.

CHAPTER 3: YOU ARE NOT SPECIAL

Developing high self-esteem became a major trend in the 1960s after research indicated that people who thought highly of themselves outperformed their counterparts who had low self-esteem. In line with this research, teachers inflated student grades, gave awards for trivial accomplishments, and often asked students to write the things that made them special. Half a century later, studies have indicated that failure is useful for developing strong minds, and feeling special means nothing if it is not backed by good reasons.

The true measure of self-esteem is not how one feels positively about himself, but how one feels about his negative aspects. Imagining success to make up for the problems you can't face is delusional; it is a high that gets you nowhere. A person with high self-esteem admits frankly to himself that he has a weakness and works on it. In the minds of entitled people, everything that happens either affirms their greatness or proves that there are people out to crush their genius. They make no meaningful improvement because in their 'special' eyes, they can do no wrong. But as is always the case, reality catches up with them sooner or later.

Things Fall Apart

Growing up, Manson was a rebellious teenager. So much so that when he was thirteen, he was expelled from school after the principal found a hidden compartment in his backpack stacked with marijuana. In the span of a few months, he had lost all his friends and his parents had divorced. In the face of seemingly unsolvable problems, Manson felt he was special (in a uniquely defective way) and subsequently took up an entitled attitude.

This entitlement played out in his early adulthood relationships. To sustain the thought that he was loved, accepted, and worthy, Manson took to chasing women, stringing unhealthy relationships, and having meaningless sex. He felt he deserved special treatment because he was awesome and everyone else wasn't. Sometimes he felt this way because he thought everyone else was awesome and he wasn't.

What he didn't realize is that the problems he had endured through his adolescence were not special: millions of other people had gone through or were going through worse. This realization would have been the first step towards dealing with his entitlement issues.

Today, emotional fortitude appears to be declining. Millennials are increasingly showing signs of emotional distress over common inconveniences like arguments with peers or low grades. It appears that the more the standards of living get better, the more people feel entitled to have even better lives.

The Tyranny of Exceptionalism

Most of life – and the people living it – is pretty much average. It takes a lot of time and energy to be exceptionally good at one thing, and most people will never be exceptional in anything at all. It is almost impossible for anyone to be an extraordinary performer in multiple areas of life.

Yet, popular media have propagated the idea that being exceptional is the new normal. With the explosion of information in the digital age, the news, jokes, or reports that get the most attention are those that show the extremes of the human condition: the scariest news, the funniest jokes, or the tales of people overcoming insurmountable challenges. Since most people are quite average, watching others accomplish exceptional feats increases their feelings of insecurity and inadequacy. Most people compensate for this sense of inadequacy by indulging in addiction or entitlement. The commercialization of exceptionalism has led people to believe that for them to matter, they need to win more awards, to take part in more philanthropy efforts, or to be more extreme.

B-b-b-but, if I'm not going to be Special or Extraordinary, what's the Point?

Celebrities, politicians, self-help gurus, and other influencers have popularized the notion that everyone is destined to be extraordinary. As average becomes synonymous with failure, people are increasingly opting to be at the extreme low of human achievement rather than be in the middle with the masses. The reasoning has been that you are as easily noticeable when you act victimized or stay at the bottom as you are at the top.

To believe that the only life worth living is a notable one is to live in a constant state of failure. People who are truly exceptional do not become extraordinary because they believe they are special but because they strive for continuous improvement. Striving for continuous improvement comes from the realization that one has yet to become great. The people who become great are the ones who acknowledge that they are average and, consequently, nurture an obsession to become better.

Key Takeaways

• The constant focus of the media on exceptional people has downplayed some simple life truths: that 99 percent of people are average, that being extraordinary does not make your life better, and that being average does not make you a failure.

• Accepting that most of your life will not be noteworthy frees you from the pressure of being the next big thing and allows you to accomplish what truly matters to you.

CHAPTER 4: THE VALUE OF SUFFERING

Three decades after the end of the Second World War, Hiroo Onoda, a lieutenant of the Japanese Imperial Army, was still fighting in the Philistine jungle, unaware that the war had long ended. Attempts by the Philistine government to draw him out with leaflets failed; he believed it was a ploy by the American government to entrap him. He fought on for so long because he had been under strict instructions not to surrender.

Years later, Onoda said that while he had spent a huge part of his life in the jungle by himself, fighting a lost war, he did not regret any of it. Onoda was able to endure his suffering because it meant something to him.

As suffering is unavoidable, it would seem that any attempt to stop suffering is a loser's game. A better strategy would be to choose the purpose for which you are ready to suffer.

The Self-Awareness Onion

Self-awareness is like an onion: it has many layers, and the more you peel, the more uncomfortable it gets. The first few layers are the ability to identify and question the emotions you feel. The deeper layers are your personal values: what you measure yourself against, how you judge others, and what you consider success or failure. This layer is the most difficult but also the most important because it determines the quality of your life.

Most people operate on a shallow level of self-awareness: they opt to chase highs and material gains rather than go through the uncomfortable process of asking themselves why they need these things. With this unending chase, the long-term problems that cause unhappiness go unresolved. The key to finding the root of your unhappiness or the source of your unending problems is to ask yourself difficult "why" questions.

The standards you use to measure your problems often define the meaning of the problems. Sometimes realizing that owning a beach house is not a metric for success, or that constant communication is not a metric for a good relationship, allows you to objectively review your feelings of dissatisfaction.

Rock Star Problems

Metallica was just about to sign its first record deal when it dropped guitarist Dave Mustaine from the band. Mustaine swore he would create a band that would be so successful that Metallica would regret its decision. In just a few years, Megadeth, the band he created, had sold over 25 million albums. Unfortunately for him, Metallica had sold 180 million albums. Despite his success, Mustaine considered himself a failure because he had not measured up the record sales of his former band.

Owing to an innate animal instinct, human beings are wired to measure their progress against that of their peers. It is not so much a question of *if* one measures his progress against that of others as it is a question of *what* metric he uses to make his comparisons. For Mustaine, success meant being more popular than Metallica.

Your values determine the standards you use to measure up against others. When your values change, your standards change, and so does the way you see your problems. Like Mustaine, Pete Best was kicked out of the Beatles just months before the band became world-famous. Three decades later, he confessed that he was happier than he would have been with the Beatles. After parting ways with the Beatles, he had nursed a depression for years but eventually got married and became a father. A loving family and a simple life became more important to him than fame and money. With this change in values, Best realized that getting kicked out of the Beatles was, in a way, a good thing.

Shitty Values

Some common values create problems that are not easy to solve. These include:

• **Pleasure**: The pursuit of pleasure (whether food, sex, or drugs) creates more anxiety and emotional instability and good feelings. With the commercialization of pleasure, people are forgetting that pleasure is the effect, not the cause, of happiness. Pleasure comes naturally when you pursue the right values.

• **Material success:** Beyond the resources you need to satisfy your basic physical needs, material gains only marginally increase your level of happiness.

• **Always being right:** The desire to be right all the time keeps you from taking on new perspectives and learning from your mistakes.

• **Staying positive:** Ignoring negative emotions prolongs their effect and perpetuates the problems behind them.

Defining Good and Bad Values

Values are good if they are based on reality, are socially constructive, and are within a person's immediate control. Honesty, charity, and standing up for others are good values because they benefit other people and are within a person's control. These are values that you can achieve internally. Popularity, dominance, or a desire to feel good all the time are unhealthy values because they are not within one's control and are difficult to ascertain.

When you prioritize unhealthy values over good values, you give more attention to the things that don't matter and that make your life worse. Self-improvement is about prioritizing healthy values

Key Takeaways

• The period you struggle through will mark some of the best years of your life because true happiness comes from solving problems.

• The difference between a good life and an unsatisfied life boils down to the values you prioritize and the metric you use to measure success and failure.

CHAPTER 5: YOU ARE ALWAYS CHOOSING

Misery comes from the view that you did not choose the problem you are dealing with or the perception that the solution is outside your control. Knowing that you chose your problems abates feelings of victimization and empowers you to solve them.

The Choice

When he was almost thirty years old, William James was unemployed, had failed at everything he had tried, and had a host of health conditions that regularly betrayed his frail body. His brother and sister were famous writers, and his father hardly missed an opportunity to express his disappointment in him. As he battled suicidal thoughts, James decided to try a thought experiment for a year, after which he would take his life. For the entire year, he was going to believe that he was fully responsible for everything that happened to him and try to change his circumstances, even if he knew failure was imminent. Thanks to the experiment, James became the most influential intellectual of his time and came to be known as the father of American psychology.

At the base of every rebirth, every growth, and every personal improvement is the realization that one is fully responsible for everything that happens in his life. You may not be in control of the external forces that impact your life, but you are always in control of how you interpret and respond to the circumstances.

"We are always interpreting the meaning of every moment and every occurrence. We are always choosing the values by which we live and the metrics by which we measure everything that happens to us."

It's impossible to not care for something. In this sense, the question is not *if* you care about something, but *what* you care for: what values do you choose, what metrics do you measure your life against?

The Responsibility/Fault Fallacy

The more responsibility you take for the things that happen in your life, the more power you have to take charge and turn everything around. Most people fail to take responsibility for their problems because they believe taking responsibility will mean taking fault. However, responsibility does not always equate to fault. If a stranger leaves a baby on your doorstep, for example, it is not your fault a baby has been abandoned. But the baby is now your responsibility.

Whereas responsibility concerns the present, fault concerns the past. You are at fault for the things you did in the past and responsible for what you do now and in the days to come. In this sense, the only person who is ever responsible for your current situation is you. Other people may be at fault for causing your problems, but only you are responsible for your problems; the way you look at, react, and address your problems is entirely up to you.

Responding to Tragedy

Regardless of the intensity of a tragedy, you are responsible for choosing how you interpret the event and react to it. You may not have chosen the tragedy – or the responsibility for coping – but you have to choose how you handle the emotional toll that comes with it. Suffering is inevitable in life, but it is up to the individual to choose the meaning of the pain.

Genetics and the Hand We're Dealt

No one chooses to be born with a genetic disadvantage, but anyone can and has to choose how he lives with the inconvenience. The behavior of someone with OCD or any other genetic deficiency may not be his fault, but he is still responsible for how he sees his situation. Like a poker house, life can deal you great or terrible cards. Great cards improve your chances of winning the hand but, ultimately, it is the choices you make throughout the game that determine if you win or lose.

Victimhood Chic

Equating responsibility to fault is tempting not only because it allows one to pass the responsibility of solving one's problems to others, but also because it gives the person blaming others a temporary high. The internet and social media have made it possible for anyone facing the slightest injustice to vent out and seek sympathy or attention from others. Feigning victimhood or expressing offense is addictive because it gives the "victim" the pleasure of knowing that he is morally superior. Outrage is especially damaging to the people who partake in it because they don't realize it's an addictive pleasure.

There is No "How"

There is no "how" to changing feelings of entitlement, victimhood, or the tendency to avoid responsibility. The only way to overcome these feelings is to choose to care about other things and values. It may sound like simple advice but it is quite difficult: you will feel uncertain about giving up old values, feel like a failure for letting go of some of your success metrics, and face rejection from the people who subscribe to your old values.

Key Takeaways

• Real growth and learning come from taking full responsibility of your problems. Success and happiness come with no worthwhile lessons.

• It is not your fault if you have an incurable disorder, had a bad childhood, or went through a scarring tragedy. However, you are responsible for moving on and making the best of your circumstances.

CHAPTER 6: YOU'RE WRONG ABOUT EVERYTHING (BUT SO AM I)

Looking back and realizing how wrong you have been about aspects of your life is a good thing because it means you have grown. When you acquire new knowledge, the information only makes you less wrong about something because growth is a lifelong process and no one really gets to the whole truth. In this sense, your goal should not be to be right but to lessen the ways you are wrong today.

When you obsess about living the "right" way, you may end up having never lived at all. Being certain about anything forestalls growth because it inhibits any attempt you make to test the waters. For most people, it is easier to put in long hours at the office, stay in a mental comfort zone, and wait for a promotion than ask for one and face the possibility that they lack marketable skills. They would rather remain quietly certain of their skills than do anything that may challenge this certainty.

Making conscious efforts to doubt your feelings, beliefs, and future possibilities is a better catalyst for growth than certainty. The positive experiences you go through today may not be all that good for your life, and the negative experiences you endure may turn out to be the most meaningful.

Architects of our Beliefs

The human brain is constantly looking for associations between experiences in order to generate meaning. While this process is designed to ease environmental interpretation, the brain often misinterprets and forgets and tends to hold on to meanings even when new evidence contradicts the meanings. For this reason, most beliefs are wrong. Even the beliefs that seem right are only less wrong than others.

Be Careful What You Believe

People tend to remember a different version of the things they experienced. As the years go by and the memory fades, the brain invents experiences to fill the memory gaps. In time, these add-ons become part of the experience that one remembers.

The human brain is always biased in that it interprets events using the values and experiences it has accumulated over the years. People interpret experiences positively when circumstances are good, and good memories become bitter when circumstances change. Your mind's priority is to fit your experiences within the realm of your beliefs, feelings, and past experiences. When you encounter a situation that does not match your past experiences, your mind invents new memories so that you can find meaning in the situation. If you are routinely exposed to negative feelings – by your personal relationships or the media – it is easy for your mind to invent negative memories and take on a victimhood attitude. Victimhood is especially easy to take on because your mind has a subconscious desire to avoid responsibility.

With memory being so unreliable and beliefs so fluid, it serves you better to trust your instinct less and question your motivations. Taking on the assumption that you are wrong all the time and approaching life with a healthy dose of skepticism is as liberating as it is a catalyst for growth.

The Dangers of Pure Certainty

Certainty may sound like a worthy value, but it often breeds insecurity. When you are certain about your job skills, nothing wreaks more havoc on your emotional fortitude than to see colleagues you consider to have inferior skills get promoted over you. With this insecurity comes despair and, subsequently, the belief that you are justified in cheating to get what you want.

Embracing uncertainty is not only comforting in an uncertain world, but it also relieves you of your judgment of yourself and others. When you accept that you don't know how attractive you are or how successful you can become, you lessen your feelings of self-loathing and envy. Accepting that you don't know much pushes you to seek learning opportunities and sets you on a course of progress and growth. You can only change your values and beliefs for the better if you admit that you are uncertain of their usefulness.

"Our values are imperfect and incomplete, and to assume that they are perfect and complete is to put us in a dangerously dogmatic mindset that breeds entitlement and avoids responsibility. The only way to solve our problems is to first admit that our actions and beliefs up to this point have been wrong and are not working."

Manson's Law of Avoidance

On his law of avoidance, Manson opines that the more something challenges the way you see yourself, the more you are going to avoid it. Your brain, which has a deep-rooted desire for comfort, views as threatening anything that stirs your perception of yourself or the world. People are as afraid of success as they are of failure because it threatens their identity.

Since beliefs precede action, you cannot overcome your personal problems until you change how you view yourself. Never finding who you really are is a good thing because it is what keeps you on the constant search for a better version of you.

Kill Yourself

The standards you use to define yourself and the stories you tell yourself are a form of self-imprisonment. When you accept that you are not who you think you are, you are free to take on new challenges, grow, and fail because you have no identity to protect. It pays off to realize that your problems are no different than those of others and to choose to measure yourself by ordinary metrics because the more you take on a narrow identity, the more change will threaten you. When you give up the idea that you are special or uniquely talented, you give up the illusion that the world owes you something.

How to Be a Little Less Certain of Yourself

To cultivate some uncertainty in your life,

• Make a habit of asking yourself if you are wrong about yourself and the meanings you generate from your experiences and entertain the thought that you could be wrong. Remind yourself that only by finding what is wrong about your life can you change for the better.

• Ask yourself what it could mean if you are wrong. Consider the values you would have to adopt to replace your current values.

• Ask yourself if being wrong would create a better or worse problem. For example, admitting that you don't know what is best for other people and acting like it can improve your relationships with others.

Key Takeaways

• The basis of change and growth is the admission that you are wrong about the meanings your mind has generated, the possibilities you see, and the values you hold.

• Embracing the uncertainty of not knowing who you are keeps you discovering and frees you to accept yourself and others.

CHAPTER 7: FAILURE IS THE WAY FORWARD

Manson graduated college at the onset of the 2007/8 financial crisis. With no savings and no real job, he stringed together odd jobs and slept on friends' sofas just to get by. In his view, he was fortunate because he started at rock bottom. Since he was already a failure, there was no fear to keep him from starting a blog and an internet business, which ultimately became a successful venture.

The Failure/Success Paradox

The level of improvement or the success you attain in something is a direct result of the number of times you have failed at it. Someone else is only better than you at something because he has failed at it more times than you. In this sense, you only succeed at the things you are willing to fail.

Most of the time, the fear of failure comes from the adoption of bad values. For example, if an artist measures success by his popularity, he faces imminent failure because the standard he uses is not within his control. Good values (such as honesty) are within one's control and are an ongoing process – they are never really achieved. When you define success by achievable values (such as buying a house or car), achieving these values leaves you feeling empty because you have solved the problem that has been the source of your drive.

Pain is Part of the Process

Most people make their most meaningful achievements when they go through seemingly insurmountable pain or adversity. Many cancer and war survivors report that their experiences made them more resilient and appreciative of the things that matter most to them. While fear and anxiety may feel like burdening emotions, they are necessary for psychological growth.

Pain forces you to assess your values and find why they are failing you. Pain forces change. Positive thinking, entitlement, or any other kind of delusional thinking that covers your problems does not inspire any change. Allow yourself to feel the pain and to act through it, not away from it.

The "Do Something" Principle

Motivation not only inspires action; it also comes from it. Your actions create the emotional inspiration and motivation you need to get things started. When you sit down and do something – even if you don't know what you are doing – the answers you need come to you. Whenever you lack the motivation to change any aspect of your life, try doing something – no matter how trivial – towards your objective. When you measure success by the slightest actions you take, any result is important and motivating. Adopting the "Do Something" principle not only enables you to stop procrastinating, but also to take up new values.

Key Takeaways

• You can generate your own inspiration and motivation by regularly showing up at your work desk, doing something – no matter how trivial – and measuring success by the action rather than the outcome.

CHAPTER 8: THE IMPORTANCE OF SAYING NO

While freedom gives you the opportunity to generate a wide range of meanings, it is not meaningful by itself. You achieve meaning when you reject the alternatives available to you and commit to a person, belief, or place because meaning comes from a depth that can only be found through commitment.

Rejection Makes Your Life Better

The self-help industry has popularized the idea that only by saying 'yes' to everything and everyone can you open yourself up to opportunities. However, if you accept everything, it means you stand for nothing; you have no values. When you lose sight of your values, you lose sight of your life's purpose.

Your life lacks direction when you avoid giving or receiving rejection. Only by rejecting alternatives can you commit to certain values or purposes and make your life meaningful.

Boundaries

Up until a century and half ago, romantic love was not the cultural craze it was today. In a way, the drama of romantic love that people pursue today is an emotional high that people use to escape their problems. Healthy love is characterized by people who take responsibility, confront their problems, and address them with each other's support. People in healthy relationships establish clear boundaries and are open to rejecting or accepting rejection by their partner. They support each other only because they want to, not because they feel obliged.

How to Build Trust

Conflict weeds out the people who are in your life for the benefits and, subsequently, breeds trust. If you are constantly trying to make your partner feel good by agreeing or doing agreeable things, your relationship will crumble without you realizing it. The pain that comes with honesty, conflict, or disagreement is the foundation of trust and intimacy in any relationship. People who are willing to say and hear 'no' from their partners keep their boundaries intact and their relationship healthy.

If trust is broken, it can only be rebuilt if the person who broke it admits that his values are not aligned with those of a healthy relationship and commits to positive change. If a husband cheats on his wife, for example, he has to admit that his impulses – or validation through sex – were more important to him than the relationship. After this self-aware admission, he has to build a track record of positive values that must be evident in the form of improved behavior.

Freedom through Commitment

More is not always better: the more options you have, the less satisfied you become with what you choose. Not only are you acutely aware of the other options you forfeited, but you also tend to second-guess your choice. Commitment may deny you a range of experiences, but it offers rich experiences of its own. You can only enjoy certain benefits if you live in one place or stay with one partner for years on end. What's more, the pursuit of more follows the law of diminishing marginal returns: each new experience adds a little less to your happiness than the last experience.

Choosing what truly matters to you and committing to it frees you from having to deal with what is trivial and unimportant. Commitment not only eases decision-making, it reassures you that what you have is good enough, and that you are not missing out on something better.

Key Takeaways

• A purposeful life lies deep beneath the surface. Only through commitment to a career, relationship, or a lifestyle can one find genuinely rich experiences.

CHAPTER 9: … AND THEN YOU DIE

When he was nineteen, Manson lost his best friend to a swimming accident and, consequently, sank into depression. After grappling with the incident for months, he realized that death was inevitable and that if he continued avoiding what was painful and uncomfortable, his life would be over before he lived it. Following this realization, he gave up his video games, weed, and cigarettes, and signed up for college courses. In his view, the tragedy was the most transformational event of his life.

Something Beyond Our Selves

People avoid talking about or acknowledging death because it is a scary void. In his book, *The Denial of Death*, Ernest Becker contends that unlike other animals, human beings are acutely aware of the inevitability of the death of their physical selves. This awareness scares them so much that they spend entire lifetimes constructing conceptual selves (buildings, books, statues, or other legacies) that will live on forever. Every conceivable human achievement – be it political conquest, art, religion, or technological innovation – and all meaning in life is the result of a deep-rooted desire to never die.

The immortality projects people pursue are, to an extent, effective in distracting them from grappling with the inevitability of their deaths. However, only by accepting the reality of death can one confront his conceptual self and choose values freely.

The Sunny Side of Death

In a way, it is the fear of life that breeds the fear of death. By confronting the possibility of death, one is able to relinquish his superficial values and focus on what really matters. As you chase fortune or fame, death is always lurking around the corner, waiting, asking what your legacy will be. In the end, the question of what mark you will leave when you die is the only question that really matters.

The source of all happiness is a concern greater than the self; it is the realization that one is a small, contributing agent in the grand scheme of things, and that one ought to make this role a central part of his life. Entitlement undermines this perspective because it pulls all attention to the self. Everyone is going to die, and this fact alone ought to make each person feel great about living and choose worthwhile values.

Key Takeaways

- The only way to overcome the fear of death is to choose and live values that go beyond serving yourself.

*** END ***

If you enjoyed this summary, please leave 5 stars and an honest review on Amazon.com!

Here are some other available titles from FastReads we think you'll enjoy:

Summary of Ego is the Enemy: by Ryan Holiday

Summary of Tribe: by Sebastian Junger

Summary of You Are a Badass: by Jen Sincero

Summary of Grit: by Angela Duckworth

Printed in Great Britain
by Amazon